Feathered Words

To Kath
best wishes
Sandra

Sandra Mary Chambers

FEATHERED WORDS

Cover Photograph – Peacock – S.M. Chambers

First Printing: 2022

ISBN: 978-1-7397105-1-4 (DREAM WELL WRITING)

DREAM WELL WRITING LTD
STAFFORDSHIRE
UNITED KINGDOM

www.dreamwellwriting.simplesite.com

A Dyslexia Friendly Publication

DEDICATION

To my husband John

FEATHERED WORDS

A collection of poetry by Sandra Mary Chambers

Sold in support of

The Midland Centre for Spinal Injuries

R.J.A.H. Hospital, Oswestry

CONTENTS

NOTE FROM THE EDITOR

Sandra and I met at Stafford Library in the autumn of 2017, when she attended a series of my poetry workshops 'The Colour of Feelings' with a focus on writing poetry as an aid to emotional wellbeing. Although having previously never written poetry, it soon became apparent that Sandra is a naturally expressive writer – with a fine attention to detail and the ability to draw the reader in to listen to every word when performing her work aloud. I remember how very moved I was on hearing the first poem that she wrote and shared at the workshop – that captured some of her experiences and emotions surrounding her husband John's accident – and how very brave I thought she was to share something so personal with strangers.

From those first workshop sessions to now, Sandra has become a hugely involved member of the local poetry scene – particularly in her voluntary role as judge at WORD Stafford over the last four years – and writes with honesty, integrity and sincerity on a wide range of topics. If tasked to write for a particular theme, I know that Sandra pours her heart and soul into exploring the topic and consequently, her work is always well researched and an absolute pleasure to read. Sandra has become a good friend over the last few years and it has been my pleasure to publish her debut collection *Feathered Words* and give a permanence to her words that is so richly deserved.

Mel Wardle Woodend
Staffordshire Poet Laureate 2019 – 2022 and
Director of Dream Well Writing Ltd

ACKNOWLEDGEMENTS

My thanks go to Mel Wardle Woodend, Staffordshire Poet Laureate, for her kindness and encouragement. She opened the door of the poetry world to me when other doors had closed. Her support in publishing this book has been greatly appreciated.

Thanks to John, my husband, for his unfailing patience with my poetry writing, and the way he has welcomed and engaged with my efforts.

Finally, last but by no means least, thank you dear reader for supporting the incredible Midland Centre for Spinal Injuries where patients with life-changing injuries and their families receive outstanding care.

INTRODUCTION

On 6th September 2016 my husband sustained a spinal cord injury. Weeks in intensive care followed, and eventually at the end of December he was transferred to the Midland Centre for Spinal Injuries at Oswestry to begin the lengthy process of rehabilitation. Finally on 27th April 2017 he was discharged.

We are very thankful for the care he received during almost eight months in hospital. There have been changes and adjustments in both our lives, in fact for the whole family. Life is different but good. Poetry writing became my new hobby, so it seems fitting that I should put my efforts to worthwhile use in creating this collection.

Thank you for buying Feathered Words. You are supporting the centre where spinal cord injury patients, their families and friends, are coming to terms with life-changing injuries, and members of staff are working with them to achieve the most positive outcomes.

Sandra Mary Chambers

PERCY THE PEACOCK

PERCY THE PEACOCK –

Artist Luke Kite, British Ironwork Centre

At the entrance to the R.J.A.H. Hospital there proudly stands a statue of a peacock. This is in memory of Percy who lived at the hospital for 22 years.

Look closely: it has been created using obsolete theatre instruments.

Benedictus

Centuries of whispered prayer
fill this churchyard,
slowly I push his wheelchair
swathes of snowdrops greet us
a vision to lift our spirits.
For months two hapless souls
trapped in the white waiting
of Critical Care,
him slipping between life and death,
against the odds
he emerged victorious.
Hesitant snowflakes
now softly anoint him,
snowdrops surround us,
little lustrous day-stars
bringers of joy
in the present moment,
signallers of hope
for a future as blank
as crisp untrodden snow.
I stop and entwine my cold fingers
in his gloved hand,
a gentle squeeze and
I am blessed.

Airborne

Your power steals the autumn day
trees shudder
crisp remaining leaves
are plucked from abandoned branches
swirl in bronze and golden eddies over pavements
form heaps in gutters.

Your power stalls the migrating bird
holds hovering
on its smooth flightpath
gently dipping, buffeting wings
no longer able to soar gracefully skywards
helpless feathers locked.

Your power transforms a playground
children change
into shrieking savages
arms outstretched feeling the force
racing on tiptoe against relentless gusts
hopeful to be airborne.

Anonypuss

Unremarkable,
a cat sitting on a fence,
just a pause from midnight mousing.
Flippin' 'eck where did that come from?
Mr Shaw never saw
your glorious tortoiseshell fur,
splendid markings for a tabby.
That werra sharp bend!
His headlamps shone out,
your eyes beamed back
luminous and large.
Bloomin' fog, a reet pea-souper.
Ideas come like a bolt
from the blue they say,
in this case a flash in the dark.
Reckon I could mek summat as like fer
road.
You crept away into the night,
an accidental hero – anonymous.
Next day Mr Shaw headed off to his workshop.

Mr Percy Shaw, born 1890 Halifax, inventor of the reflective road stud known as Cats' Eyes

Beddgelert

Storm clouds loom large and low
over Welsh mountains,
Prince Llewellyn returns to his stronghold
scene of carnage awaits,
pools of bright blood
on the stone floor
glisten in the candlelight,
stained shredded coverlet
empty cradle
a sight to torture his heart
drain his soul.

Gelert, faithful hound, trusted friend
limps yelping into the chamber
blood dripping from his jaws
matting his coat,
lightning flash of anger
sword drawn from gleaming scabbard
Llewellyn slashes the air
in fury swings a fatal blow,
“Murderous creature!”
his shout echoes like thunder
around the Great Hall.

Sinking to his knees
Llewellyn howls at the treachery
suffocated by the horror,
the loss of his princeling son
his pride, his joy,
he strides out to the castle walls
attempting to breathe
he spies a motionless black shape
mighty wolf mauled to death
by brave Gelert
defending the child.

Remorseful he turns back,
a faint cry breaks the deadly silence,
his beloved child
lies in the shadow of an oaken chest
safe and sound.

Beddgelert – Gelert's Grave

Now was brave Gelert, honoured by his master, buried in that Welsh valley?

Did that beloved child grow to walk in his thankful father's footsteps?

In every legend a truth lies there embedded,

here 'Think it possible that you may be mistaken.'

Bloom

Unfurl your petals
bold bright poppy
attention seeker
all eyes on you
in tangled flowerbed.

Live in the moment
razzle dazzle red
petals neverlasting
life brought to an end
too quickly.

Maybe the gentle kiss
of warm summer breeze
or the fleeting caress
of a blackbird's wing
will steal our joy.

Cherish the Day

Eager outstretched arms
wind around me,
low crushing hug
your rugby-tackle of love,
stumbling, we laugh and dance crazily.

Sun-dazzled adventurers
your hot little hand in mine,
we cross new-mown meadows
fresh greenness fills the air,
you break free, wildly racing ahead.

Eagle-eyed you gently
coax a ladybird
from the spike of grass,
proudly proving you've mastered
counting her spots with precision.

We straddle rough logs
imitating the sounds of a train,
repeating the journey
again and again,
toots, chugs, whistles, for your delight.

You offer, insist I take
your last sherbet lemon,
stuck fast in the corner
of the crumpled paper bag.
You beam as I receive the supreme accolade.

Chisel

National Memorial Arboretum, Alrewas, Staffordshire

In this green heart of Mercia
climb the hill of grief and prayer,
looming walls of Portland stone
form the stark vision standing there,
shafts of sunlight lie in wait.

True the deadliest war long ended,
yet new names are carved with precision
for bodies blasted into oblivion,
chip, chip, chisel cleaves the silence
sharp white stone fragments fly.

Once armed forces, columns marching,
boots tramping, field guns pounding
bombs exploding, retreat sounding,
now ordered columns honour the fallen
in this garden of sorrow, a betrayal of peace.

Unceasing deaths, still millions mourn,
haunting horror of blank stone walls
awaiting future desecration
more tears of anguish, more pools of blood
we stare at this abomination.

Chip, chip, chisel cleaves the silence.

Collateral Damage

Strangers will be at the door
my clock is not my own,
the calendar punctuated with dates
for testing, assessing, reviewing,
our new mad social whirl.

I free you from confinement,
lower cold rails of hospital bed
dispose of hygiene sheets and catheters,
this bold brave world of ours,
lever your body to sitting position.

Next the other women make their entrance,
criminally cheerful for that hour
remove you to mechanical care,
hands perform tasks in zones
of our uncharted intimacy.

Excluded I hear you engage in tales
water cascading cleansing purifying,
now I am divorced, discarded,
let me take out the bin
attempt twisting open the marmalade.

I iron the clothes of your new uniform
jogging bottoms, t-shirt,
foreign in name and nature
for hands that cannot function as before
try to remember you in smart shirts and chinos.

You pulled me onto the dancefloor
as I laughed protesting at being first,
teasing me, twirling me underarm.
Now I spin with poems in my head,
the other women make your bed.

With thanks through my forced smile
they close the door on our altered union,
rituals of personal care render you exhausted
you doze in your wheelchair battle-weary,
I surrender, yet love remains undefeated.

Colossus

The coldest
the windiest
the driest
place on Earth
Antarctica
magnificent ice mass of
chiselled shimmering beauty
where glittering glaciers flow
and icebergs float free.

Far below
tell-tale warm waters
signal doomsday,
shrinking ice shelves
widening fissures,
glaciers are creeping   creaking   cracking
glaciers are shifting   sliding   splitting
one trillion tonnes of ice on the move
the Colossus breaks free.

Day 1 of 1137

T.V. quizmaster is drowned by the sound
of the radio successfully competing for attention
with songs from the shows,
decibels not conducive to polite conversation,
or any conversation, but there is none.
The answers no one knows.
Some enchanted evening trills the songbird,
but this is quite the opposite I suppose.

Some enchanted evening, you may see a stranger.
In this room there are many, and many doing strange things,
opposite a woman wears odd slippers,
nearby one douses her false teeth in her tea,
another attempts the Herculean task
of keeping between the lines in a child's colouring book,
next to me a highly agitated lady......my mother,
uniformed strangers too, not a name badge in sight,
yet I am the stranger here and you don't belong.

Some enchanted evening, you may see a stranger across a crowded room.
This room is crowded, jam-packed,
walking frames, wheelchairs, tea trolley, hoist, medicine trolley,
perimeter of elderly residents, fragile shells of themselves

half asleep and sleeping, lifetimes of long-forgotten memories.
Sickly smell of evening meal lingers, you don't belong here.

Care assistant perched on a table gazes blankly at a huge T.V. screen,
inspects her fingernails for chips, checks her phone,
how many minutes to handover?
Wishing her life away.
My mother is calmer now
I plant a kiss upon her parchment cheek,
emergency respite, assessment, what next?

In the corner a lost soul curled in foetal position,
slim, auburn-haired barely middle-aged
and she is.....singing. Beautifully
Some enchanted evening.
Every word remembered
there was no radio,
the cruelty of early onset dementia.

Inward swell of tears, I leave, but not for the last time.
And somehow you know, you know even then
that somehow you'll see here again and again.

Departures

From here I can go anywhere I wish,
I need no suitcase bulging at the clasps,
no need of map, folded and unfolded,
nor compass needle dalliance.
For I am surrounded
endless destinations to explore,
lives to live again,
time and space colliding
in the evergreen forest of volumes,
magic maze of words,
imaginarium of bright ideas.

Through this portal into other worlds
all manner of possibilities,
all manner of improbabilities,
tangled mysteries to unwind,
challenging adventures to complete,
lost on lonely mountaintops,
sheltering in cities scarred by war,
hiding with souls disturbed by darkness.
At least until five thirty prompt,
when I must snatch my companions for the week,
head home, from the last library standing.

Earthstruck

First woman on the moon?
An honour, I told the farewell press team,
lunar sanctuary of celestial peace
far from our world's chaos and clamour.

The full Earth beams down,
walls borders divisions invisible,
cosmic bauble spinning, fragility shining through
this boundless universe, black shroud of mysteries.

From a distance all is perfection;
pollution, extinction, climate catastrophe, just words.
The deadly impact of human activity
imperceptible, unbelievable.

In wonderment I gaze
on that warming globe in our galaxy,
thoughts of my child, light of my life,
two hundred thousand miles away.

Untrue blue of oceans, white swirling clouds
hold me transfixed,
planet of seven billion souls
beauty betrays your difficult birth.

Gifts of oxygen, water, temperature conducive
for life-forms, nurtured in perfect unity,
Humankind's true privilege
being born into that heaven.

Upon this bleak barren moonscape,
I contemplate the fate of my progeny,
neglect and greed extinguishing our light of Life,
and pray for Earth's salvation.

Eco Worrier

Putting recyclables in the bin
the first cardinal sin.
Showering for too long
drenching yourself, so wrong.
Thermostat set too high
carbon dioxide reach for the sky.
Where we could easily walk we take the car
journeys near or journeys far.
Spending money on clothes never worn
reuse, recycle, repair the torn.
Allowing food to go off, fridge full past date
use by, best before. Just carefully rotate.
Leaving lights on in an empty room
flick the switch forget the gloom.
Bags for life not being used
planet's resources being abused.
Using the dishwasher nearly empty
wait until you have plenty
leaving water running while brushing your teeth
the things we do beggar's belief
let's share, spare, care, conserve
leave the children a world they deserve.

Ensnared

Bronzing on deserted beach
muscles toned and defined,
he admires his myriad of tattoos
intricate ink-filled lines;
loathsome viper coiled along his arm,
jaunty mermaid sits upon his chest,
galleon, tiger, scorpion and all the rest.

No regrets, well maybe one
her name across his heart,
he loved, lied and cheated, now smirks that she is gone.

The tide turns, and strangely
inked wrist chains tighten,
links of metal, cold and hard,
dig into his flesh to frighten.
Terror as he feels the viper's forked tongue
tickle menacingly as it slithers up his arm,
eerie sea songs echo causing him more alarm.

Before him a malodorous mermaid wails,
murderous glare from her green glassy eyes,
tendrils of long wet hair like trailing rats' tails.

Riding high on the waves
three-masted galleon in the bay,
scorpion dances across clear skin,
viper crushes its prey.
The siren winds endless hair tightly around
his form, like a spider with a doomed fly,
cold scaley tail smacks his legs, he gives a helpless cry.

With all her power she drags him out into the sea,
fiery eyes, bloody fangs, the tiger roars deafeningly.
And in the sand an invisible hand scrawls...... her name.

Escape Route

Twenty-nine permitted reasons
for leaving home
this is not one,
we are suffocating
at home the oxygen seems all used up
semi-conscious our brains are bruised
from government briefings
battered by statistics of death and disease
we struggle
to counterbalance the overwhelming gloom,
crushed beneath the weight
of shielding and self-care.

Driving down deserted streets
we note the absence of litter
gardens tended more carefully
pavements heaped with autumnal drifts, surely not?
Where were those summer months?

Feel the freedom of day release greeting us
where an expanse of lush fields
stretches towards the horizon
to challenge the smothering skies,
over the brow of the hill

spy the steely grey reservoir,
we turn to park at the water's edge,
glorious gold of an explosive sunset takes us by surprise
clouds scattering across pink blooms of early evening
the heavens are alive and well!

Florabundance

My garden sanctuary
where in my solitude
flowers call to me,
morning joy, evening consolation.

Poppies stay a while longer
your tissue paper perfection
cheers me beyond words.
Glow amidst garden greenery
delicate pink petals
speak imagination and success,
prepare to fall from the whisper of the wind
close encounter with a cat.
A brief life but a dazzling one,
know I shall mourn your loss, poppy blooms.

Foxgloves, create pink and white magic,
summon fairies to my garden,
forget your poison, abandon alchemy,
spread enchantment on shadowy banks
where waving wands dance to and fro.
Cast spells, change sparrows' dustbowl
to verdant corner,
dandelions and nettles into wine,

creeping caterpillar transform to flying peacock.
Foxgloves bewitch.

Morning glory, love in vain,
tenacity and tenderness in all things,
leaves winding clinging.
Heavenly blue lapis lazuli,
angelic trumpets sounding
flowers surprising.
From those tiny soaking seeds
skywards you grew,
why did I doubt you?
Glorious.

In my solitude
flowers call to me,
morning joy, evening consolation.
A language understood.

Flotsam

We are at a safe distance,
wind whipping our hair
icy rain pelting us at the cliff-top,
cracks showing, cracks growing
waves smash below
intent on swallowing what was
our home, our home.

Remember the shelves you sawed in the garage?
You used a spirit level,
oh so professionally,
to make sure they were absolutely level
we were impressed by your attention to detail,
now they tip perilously towards the ocean,
the books we hurriedly packed crammed into boxes.

Curtain rails or poles?
We dithered that day in B and Q
should it matter a jot
now the lot is destined to take a dive?
Curtain rings rattle as the wind howls,
nets billow like sails while the sea growls,
our home, our home.

We spent evenings discussing flooring,
better quality would last I said,
value brand leaves money in our pockets you argued.
Did it really matter what kind
now we have left it all behind?
Lifetime guarantee on the rubble-strewn beach.

Four walls and a roof over our heads
'A view to die for' you said.
Those walls privy to our passions,
privy to our petty quarrels
now gaping, our lives exposed
like a dolls' house abandoned by a petulant child,
our home, our home.

By night the human chain
moved our belongings in the rain,
our lives dismantled with urgency
no bubble wrapping china,
just snatch and grab
like scavenging car-booters
but we were glad of it.

Home, if only you could take flight
swirl and whirl like a seagull
soaring in those easterly gales,

swoop and settle in a safe sodden field.

I would open the front door, put the kettle on, and make a nice cup of tea,

BUT we are watching, waiting,

      we are at a safe distance,

our broken hearts already in pieces at the bottom of the cliff.

Hemsby, Norfolk. March 2018

Foundling

Surrendering to the freezing dread of night
she steps out,
about her head white swirls of breath.

Gas lamps glimmer in the frosty air
rooftops sparkle,
window- panes opaque with ice, dead-eyed.

Numb fingertips clasp tightly
the ragged bundle,
layers of torn blankets swaddle a tiny body.

Worn boots trudge along icy pavements
between towering factories,
past frozen canal basin, ghostly narrowboats.

Desperate tear-streaked face
heart racing, body weak,
a midnight chime disturbs the silence.

Heat of her lover's passion
a chapter closed forever
by his cold-hearted denial of their love.

Clutching her secret never to be told
she leans against ancient oak
the door creaks open, sanctuary.

Gently she places her off-spring
by the altar steps
moon gleams through stained glass.

She rips a button from her frock
by way of foundling's token,
as surely as she plucks out her own heart.

One kiss, as soft as a falling rose petal
and she has gone,
surrendering to the freezing dread of night.

Fountain of Youth

Shimmering sequins of water droplets
rain down upon me
as my toes touch ancient stonework.
I have found you!
Fountain of youth, let me bathe
rivulets running
through silvered silken strands
into my ears, sounds sharpen
showers cool and reviving
splash over me
every gnarled spot touched
caressed by sparkling water
spilling across tense shoulders
gushing between
my once-suckled breasts
furrowed frown is smoothed
feet soothed eager to dance
dizzying pirouettes of joy,
creaking elbows and knees
tingle with blessed relief
cascades roll down
bent back is eased
knots released
turkey scrag exchanged

for swan's neck elegance,
the blue embroidery threads
on thighs erase erased
worries of age and ages float
away from where this fountain plays
tinkling sounds, watery thoughts
I will lose the love of my life
offspring will never have been
all will be undone
learning, skills, experience dissolved
I drown in that knowledge.
Tell Herodotus the trade-in
is questionable
but I no longer have
the wisdom to choose.
I cup my hands and slowly sup.

Galanthus

Pearly-white pendants
dance to the tune
of the winter wind.

Your spikes of green
strong enough to push
through firm frozen ground.

Surprising snowdrops
clarion call
to the promise of spring.

Cheering the coldest heart,
leaving the world asleep
a little longer.

Glimpse

Beneath the willow boughs
watchful waiting by water's edge
tranquillity my mantle,
cluster of bank side burrows opposite
holds me transfixed.
Willing them to come alive with your shrill song,
rapid wing beats, straight flight path
low over lazy river flow,
dipping dazzling flash at lightning speed,
propelled from crumbling chambers
flecked feathers rich electric blue
or maybe sheen of oil-spill green,
undercarriage burnt amber orange,
plunging with precision for silvery sticklebacks.
Your shy emergence I await with camera poised.

From nowhere life-lustre arrow
fires past, nanoseconds of brilliance
shutter speed loses to your avian dexterity
kingfisher, you precious jewel of a bird,
spark of life to treasure, never capture.

Glory

Harps stay silent, trumpets cease
in this glorious creation
art deco song in Paradise
angel face man-made perfection.

Pearly opalescent eyes pity
mortals foolish, mortals wise
sun-kissed heavens shining bright
above our angry cloud-filled skies.

Glass as crisp as sculptured ice
moulded wings majestic white
enfold troubled spirits in a trice
shimmering gleams of ethereal light.

Vision bloomed in widow's grief
a precious memorial unique
spurred by love, loss and belief
the glass church by Rene Jules Lalique.

Crystal angel looms serene
protector, guardian, gentle guide,
glass altar, font, cross and screens
marvels to behold inside.

Some stand in awe and wonder there
whilst others kneel and pray
man or God can touch the soul
Art transcends Time brings joy this day.

Written in response to the Angel from the Lady Chapel St. Matthew's Church, Millbrook, Jersey created by Rene Lalique. Commissioned by Florence Boot, Lady Trent in memory of her husband Jesse Boot 1815-1932.

Green Requiem

By the muddy canals of Xochimilco,
weird and wonderful
axolotl,
salamander prized by the Aztec kings
steeped in mythological lore
magician-like master of regeneration.
plagued by polluted waters,
little walking fish
your feathery gills flap no more,
Mexico mourns you.

In the tropical forests of El Yunque,
green and gorgeous
Amazon parrots.
A million wingbeats silenced in the treetops,
changing climate brought catastrophe,
hurricanes hit your habitat.
Dazzling squawking birds,
your turquoise-tipped wings fan forlornly.
Puerto Rico mourns you.

On the golden shores of Kapota Island,
mighty and majestic
sperm whale,

your brain larger than any on Earth.
Now butchered by curious villagers
thirteen pounds of obscene plastic in your gut
one hundred and fifteen plastic cups.
Deep-diving ancient submariner
never again will you power through the ocean,
Indonesia mourns you.

In the newspaper I read today,
startling and shocking,
these three reports of loss,
creatures who slithered, swooped and swam,
beauteous and incredible,
across the surface of the globe
disappearing and nearing extinction.
Will they stare accusingly from fading pages in a book?
Nature's cry for help, the ceaseless song
echoing around the world.

Heligan Spring

Sky of rose-tint-dappled dawn
bitter chill of early morn,
awakening from her loamy bed
the Mud Maid stirs and lifts her head,
peers with periwinkle eyes
at proud Kernow's lost paradise.

Next she trips through woodland glade
where Cornish pixies serenade,
lightly steps twixt spring bulbs bold
orange, lilac, shimmering gold
of sunlight shafts' warming glow
on dewdrop-jewelled grass below.

Majestic tree ferns line her way
on this most magical fine spring day,
seeking Jack-in-the-Green her vital quest
from which she will never ever rest,
for Lord and Lady must dance together
else nature's gentle joys be lost forever.

Just when she thought all was lost
she finds him hiding in a copse,
tinkling laughter in the trees

teasing smile caught on the breeze,
across his brow leaf buds curl
adorn him now ‘fore leaves unfurl.

New life they breathe into earth, water, air
everything that’s dormant there,
as they dance, delight, skip and twirl
through sweet-scented confetti-blossom swirl,
nature’s perfection is re-arranged
enchantment heralds the season’s change.

High Frequency

Wings beat on your skin,
birds flit back and forth
silently
nest building.

Our bed beneath the open window
warm breeze lifts the curtains,
shadows quiver
in dappled sunlight.

Your lips move,
feathered words of love
perplexing me,
incomprehensible.

They fly around the room,
I feel their soft touch,
smile, but
do not confess.

They have fallen into the well
of silence,
sadly lost to me with
        children's voices

foreign lilts
distant bells
hum of insects
the alarm clock.
'Listen to the birds!' you delight
but no birds sing for me,
I nod to please you
keep up the pretence.

Fast forward to the morning
I came home,
the shock of gravel
crunching underfoot.

Astonished by our hedgerow
exploding with birdsong,
knowing your tender whisperings
were lying in wait.

How to Stargaze in Winter

Ideal those Christmas socks
perhaps all three pairs
and a woolly hat plus earmuffs
think extremities
gloves
insulated if possible
remember layers of layers
a flask of hot soup
is a good plan
waterproof boots
preferably with furry linings
a map of the night sky
a torch to read
the map
a spare battery for the torch
a compass for lost souls
chocolate
a good friend
for a warm hug in sub-zero conditions.

Now venture forth under the clear crisp night sky
or
simply switch off the light
and make do
with a cosy armchair
in the conservatory.

Incantations on the M6

Siren threatens
blue lights flash,
driving rain
kick of side wind
slalom of road works,
early September return
of caravans and campervans,
I am losing you
I am losing you,
let me hold you fast
in the light of our love.

Windscreen wipers'
determined swipes
clear spray
from rumbling lorries,
my heart thumps
in quick time
beating for us both,
stay with me
stay with me,
let me hold you fast
in the light of our love.

Distant blue haze,
siren fades,
we have never parted before
without a kiss goodbye.

Kwame's Christmas

Excitement rustles through paper chains
twinkles in foil icicles above corridors
the chosen ones delve hastily into a box
enchantment scatters over the hall floor
shimmering gold and silver,
Kwame watches curiously
as they decorate sharp spikes of green
like no tree he has ever seen,
one girl tiptoes for the topmost branch
holding a star aloft,
gently he takes it to fix in place
remembering the starriest of nights,
gazing up, wedged into that crowded dinghy
cold, frightened, hungry.

Morning class focus on fractions
quiet head-bowed reluctance,
fourteen days to Christmas!
Suddenly a wild shriek of delight
Kwame rushes from the room
out alone into the playground
laughs and sings in his own language,
spins, like a dervish, arms outstretched
in the pristine flurry of flakes

snow settles on his tight curls
head thrown back, open-mouthed
crystals melt on his tongue,
thirty pairs of eyes stare
from tinselled classroom windows,
shocked by his manic exit
impressed by his loud jubilation,
the first snowfall of winter
the only one he has ever seen.
Together the children cheer
  for snowy days to come,
  for Christmas just around the corner,
  for Kwame's dance of joy.

Love Song for a Broken Man

Let me enfold you in a giant cocoon
of gossamer softness,
have Atlas arms to scoop you up
cradle you, place you in a man nest
of goose feathers,
safe in strong branches of an oak,
let me be your fearless sentinel
singing you to sound sleep with lullabies.

And when you wake, all confusion gone,
delirium history, pain will be vanquished.
We shall tumble on to our own big bed
cascading feathers kiss our blessed bodies,
time to embrace,
celebrate our reunion,
laugh at the nonsense of our lives,
dance on the ceiling of our imagination.

Nevermore chasing ambulances in the driving rain,
losing myself in anonymous corridors,
catnapping on plastic chairs,
dining by permission of vending machines,
day after day after hapless day my numb vigil,
no more / end of / finis
it would all stop   in a good way
our lives re-booted, carefree, whole.

Mariana

Mariana they have named you
your strange beauty hidden six miles deep,
fathoms of octopus inky blackness
drowned by Pacific's precious vastness
your scythe-like scar cuts the seabed
'The deepest place on Earth' I've read.

If in my imagination I could dive,
explore your trough to find alive,
poisoned amphipods on the ocean floor,
scavenging the depths for ever more.
King Neptune and his Queen Salacia weep
to witness the destruction of the deep,
white horses pull their chariot aloft
surging past waste in the ocean tossed.
a realm once pristine, safe, remote,
now five trillion plastic pieces float.

If in my wildest dreams I could plunge,
through grim polluted waters lunge,
toxic globules to swiftly wrench,
from helpless marine life in your trench.
before mighty Neptune's powers terrify,
"Destroy our kingdom at your peril" his cry,

strikes his sacred trident with an angry roar,
commands, “Mankind, no more! NO MORE!”
Wild oceans crash, high seas wreak havoc
three hundred million tonnes of plastic.

Mariana they have found you,
your dark secrets hidden six miles deep,
no habitat safe, no creature free
of plastic particles from the sea.
Robotic submarines spied that degradation,
humanity’s ultimate shame...your violation.

Midnight Mass

In the belfry mince pies and a drop of sherry
waiting for the ringers to conclude,
by ancient doorway the vicar
scans the throng for familiar faces.
This is the first time I will join
the flock at midnight mass.

Turning my back on home tonight,
empty of laughter and merriment
except for rows of cards, season's greetings,
sympathetic sentences grace a few,
gathering the robins together
fleetingly lifted my sunken spirits.

Hurrying towards the moonlit church,
shop windows shock me with dazzling jollity,
flickering fairy lights dance in the wind
on the swaying village tree.
The world is celebrating, I did not notice.
For weeks I have been with you in solitary.

Memories flow; fun with our young children,
romantic celebrations just us two,
family gatherings when parents were alive.

How blessed we have been,
Christmas after Christmas,
gifts of love, peace and joy in abundance.

Now let me be where there is light from candles,
feel warmth from humanity packed into pews,
find Hope surrounds like a comforting blanket.
When bells fall silent I sit amongst strangers,
close my eyes, picture you in that hospital bed,
my only certainty – tonight was Christmas Eve.

Mother Earth

Mother Earth is sighing,
can't they hear?
Climate change denying
consumers excess buying
waste that's mystifying
Mother Earth is sighing.

Mother Earth is weeping,
don't they care?
Millions who are needy,
whilst others are so greedy
but most just feel uneasy
Mother Earth is weeping.

Mother Earth is wailing
won't they act?
Pollution laws are failing
noxious fumes inhaling
complacency prevailing
Mother Earth is wailing.

Mother Earth is dying,
can't they see?
Riverbeds are drying

crop failures terrifying
problems multiplying
Mother Earth is dying.

Mother Earth is praying,
hear her prayer,
plastic tide start turning
fossil fuels stop burning
Humankind start learning
Mother Earth is praying.

New Year's Eve

Caught in the vortex between old year and new,
her maelstrom of misery,
dismal past, bleak future,
tonight she shivers coatless,
departure sudden, destination unknown
she needs to stop the pain
of love, of loss, of longing,
cyborg-like she tramps through the night-time town.

Blank-faced boarded up shops surround,
glare from estate agent's windows dazzle,
prim neat little houses, prim neat little lives.
dank rowdy wide-open taverns
smoke from their door-step refugees
swirls across the pavement,
shoulders shaking with sobs she proceeds
oblivious to the revellers' rude remarks.

Golden balloon glows in the night sky
tethered to the festive lamp-post
like a confused sun,
distant fireworks burst and crackle,
bells fall silent, despair tightens its stranglehold
she heads towards the railway bridge,
clambers on to the stone parapet,
a gentle hand touches her shoulder, "Are you O.K. Love?"

Next of Kin

Critical Care September 2016

Lift descending into uncharted depths,
immersion into the white waiting world
stifled yawns
muffled sobs
silent prayers,
the chink of white china on the comfort tray.

The waiting room of the despairing dispossessed.
one cradles the Koran,
another scans the tabloid trivia,
most gaze into space,
Why? What if? What next?
The future now as blank as winter's clouded moon.

Then it is bedside time,
I venture past porcelain patients.
Mysterious machinery sounds sudden alarm and threat,
tenuous links with life surround me,
ventilators pump, intravenous fluids drip,
nasal tubes dribble nutrients into helpless bodies.

My hands sanitised to touch you
lifeless, horizontal in your new white sterile world

yet the monitor contradicts,
rigid collar holds your chiselled head like a vice
fans whir constantly, wires and pipes snake around you
the nurse makes her observations in silence.

Life-changing injuries
hurtle us into the void of uncertainty,
uproot, trample, tear down our cosy citadel,
others come and go I know not where,
I remain, I hear that final swish of curtains yet again,
next of kin for hours cling to the chalky cliffs of their hope.

Wearily I go alone into the cold night,
the pearly moon, the distant stars
peer down upon my fears,
like they have done on countless others over years
lives suddenly seized, fed through the snatching jaws of a shredder,
in pieces now, impossible to stick or stitch back together.

Nightprowlers

The nightprowlers circle
in the dimmed light,
the nightprowlers converge
in the silence,
disturbed only by the corridor click clacking
of purposeful walking in sensible shoes.

Trolley of coffee, cocoa, malted milk
they gather around sharing
tales of overturned lives,
the runaway sleeping under the stars
the baby abandoned in a bus shelter
the overnight drive into oblivion.

Finally he bows his head to recollect his story
of exceptional musical talent,
flute playing surpassing James Galway,
naturally he purchased the finest instrument
that money could buy in that city store,
the worries came thick and fast.

Being the wealthiest man in Britain
hiring bodyguards was the wise thing to do,
expensive but necessary,
fearing robbery at knifepoint or kidnap,
living life in high definition
heightened awareness wreaking havoc.

In the vice-like grip of points of reference
thoughts, ideas, fast and furious,
he had not had time to take the flute from its box
when the police came
had not played a note,
which was just as well.

The nightprowlers listen
as the dawn breaks
the nightprowlers nodding
all know how the tale ends,
the medicine trolley rattles closer
ready to dispense sanity.

Obituary for a Childhood

Sadly Childhood passed away,
through wildflower dolly-mixture meadows.

Grazed knees, scuffed sandals
bamboo cane, net and jar
incessant hum of insects,
relentless birdsong, fluttering butterflies.
endless sunshine,
sky an untrue blue,
untamed hedgerows
woven with wild roses and convolvulus.

Fishing accompanied by chattering friends,
shimmering stream winks at us
emerald weeds swirl in the flow
teeming with sticklebacks and minnows,
tangled banks of cow parsley and pink campion.
immeasurable happiness,
timeless days
fondly remembered.

Odeon 1961

Fingers snap, feet tap,
tension fills the air
eyes coldly stare
asphalt under feet
rival gangs meet
Bernstein's glorious score kicks in
my all-time favourite film begins.

Fingers snap, feet tap,
wire mesh surrounds
dismal dark playgrounds
New York City rocks
downtown hatred shocks
youths' amazing leaps and dives
hiding weapons sharpened knives.

Fingers snap, feet tap,
dancing dynamite
explodes into the night
jazz and ballet fuse
unexpected moves
shout and scream power and treat
from strutting Sharks or swaggering Jets.

Fingers snap, feet tap,
energy of youth
vile words of raw truth
hear the tribal beat
feel anger's boiling heat
love and hate
lie in wait to seal the tragic lovers' fate.

On Visiting The National Gallery

Room sixty-one
I know my way
the magnet is Raphael
divine love captured in
Madonna of the Pinks
oil on wood
intended for prayer and contemplation
she delights in her darling boy
proffers dianthus,

all mothers' love divine
the infant's downy head
just like one I nuzzled years ago
as I wrapped myself
around her restless sleep
exhausted,
brushwork shows the softness
of plump unstepped feet
that once kicked in utero
as those I squeezed
so gently
in the darkness
holding her quietly breathing beating body
my precious parasite
our tear-streaked faces touched,

again and again the artist paints
the mystical union of the Christ-Child
and his besotted mother,
glorious succession of Madonnas
hues of vermilion, verdigris, malachite, ultramarine
depict voluptuous Renaissance womanhood
offspring in fresh perfection,
palette never recorded her like an empty husk
drained, distraught,
brain struggling to catch
racing thoughts,
wild notions leading
to the forcible wrench apart
of mother and child.

Otherworld

Four thousand alien silhouettes
once loomed across a murky skyline
bulbous brick-built bodies
hid pulsating fiery hearts
monsters in the realm of Hades.

Towering stacks rose above rooftops
tiers of smog-swaddled terraces
dwellings for souls condemned
to earn an honest crust
toiling in fumes or choking dust.

Hellfire's improbable creations
worked from clay coal flint
chinking china clunking crocks
born in bustling pot banks
destined to circle the globe.

Saggers, jaw-crushers, jolleys, jiggers,
strange words rang out where
hard graft of the potters
earned rewards with curses
in their dismal otherworld.

Silence now for clogs on cobbled yards
forlorn factories deserted
manufacturing's miasma has gone
surviving bottle ovens stand proud
monuments in the city of six towns.

Radiogram

Walnut box stands silently
in the bay window,
nearly as tall as me,
when Grandpa lifts the lid
I tiptoe to peep in
watch the turntable spin,
mesmerised,
the music trickles down
to my feet,
I tap my own dance on the lino.

Today everyone has gone,
gone to work,
I play on the floor in silence.
From the kitchen
I hear the squelch, splash, squelch
of the ponch thrashing, pounding
the laundry in the dolly tub,
later I will help turn the mangle.
The steam swirls in
as Grandma opens the door,
I smell the suds,
she hurriedly dries her hands,
as red as the roses on her floral pinafore

edged with rick rack.
I love that word rick rack.
She tunes in the wireless
returning to the kitchen in a trice,
busy, busy, always busy,
but she never forgets quarter to two.

I clamber into the armchair
next to the radiogram,
it swallows me.
“Are you sitting comfortably?” asks the wireless,
familiar nursery rhymes
for me to sing along,
a story to lose myself in
painting pictures in my head,
spellbound by sound,
I enter a world of cockleshells
and silver bells.

Reflection

Kneeling to gaze into the deep dark pool
he does not see the fish with sparkling scales
darting to and fro
nor crane poised elegantly at the water's edge
nor dancing dragonflies skimming the surface
just his own reflection
Narcissus mirrored in the clear still water
transfixed by his beauty unsurpassed
glossy locks tumbling over fine brow
glowing skin, sun-kissed from hunting days.

In the shadows Echo grieves
for her unrequited love
while Goddess Nemesis bides her time
her curse holds him captive
beloved of himself
until in death a narcissus blooms
strangely blue as his azure eyes.

Focussed on her phone
held to seek the perfect angle
perfect light, perfect beauty
she does not hear the birdsong
or see the friendly faces in the park

oblivious to the array of flowers
blossoming roses, climbing clematis

unaware of the smell
of soft green grass freshly cut
butterflies flutter by unnoticed
blonde hair extended
frames her face
bold brows hover
above improbable lashes
curling the unseeing eyes
her full lips peach melba shade
do not move to say hello how are you
but pout to place a frozen kiss
on her own ideal image, a caricature
for the transient bloom of youth is lost
and in the park a narcissus petal falls
Goddess Nemesis smiles.

Rest In Peace

Tell me a joke Dad why don't you?
It's what you want to do.
I know it's hard to keep a straight face,
being so still just doesn't suit you.

    Tell me a joke why don't you?
    Just a wisecrack or two.
    You've been here in this chapel for quite a while,
    just sit up now and make me smile.

Me, I've come here to thank you
I was always too late it's true
you had such high hopes of me
perhaps disappointment was all you could see

    leather satchel you bought me
    but homework not done
    grand hockey stick
    though games never won

fancy fountain pen too
gold nib broken so soon.
I should have aimed for the stars,
but I gazed at the moon.

    Tell me a joke Dad why don't you?
    I'd love to hear just one more
    me, I want to say I love you
    why didn't I say it before?

You taught me to love poetry
you taught me proverbs galore
honesty is the best policy
so I will say it just once more

thank you for being my Dad
and all that you did for me
thank you for love and kindness and care
for books to read and knowledge to share

a joy in language you gave me
your sense of the absurd
your love of nature, the open air,
wanting to wander everywhere.

Well Dad I'm still waiting
what was it you wanted to say?
I'm waiting here with a tear in my eye
last words are important
so please won't you try?
I can see it is on the tip of your tongue
say it out loud and then I'll be gone

'Why did the spirit cross the road, why?...
*To get to the other side'....*Goodbye.

Seashell

Seawater drips from my fingertips,
sand grains cling to my damp toes,
glittering dancing slippers.
Taking a single fragile pearly shell from the water's edge,
its gentle serrations imprinting the sand,
I clamber rough steps
from this perfect beach
to you, for you.

King-like you gaze from your parapet
surveying our wondrous realm,
smelling the sea, hearing the heaving waves,
inaccessible expanse of paradise,
my outstretched palm gifting you the ocean
in a tiny seashell.

An African Praise-Poem in honour of
Sir David Attenborough

Hail! Great silver-crowned king,
wise man of the lush green forests,
burnt golden plains,
glistening ice sheets,
deep oceans blue,
demi-god of the natural world.

Hail! David Attenborough,
towering intellect
with thirty-two degrees,
observations of the animal kingdom unsurpassed.
Many moons ago,
trekking to discover
the fearsome Komodo dragon,
astonishing displays by birds of paradise,
all in black and white,
up to present day revelations,
explosions of colour
on our blue planet
where vanishing creatures
struggle to survive.
Do whales weep? Gorillas cry?
Do polar bears tread a sorrowful path?

In your honour named species
of daisy, lizard, fossil, beetle,
shrimp, spider, butterfly.

Globe-trotter extraordinary,
most travelled human in history...probably.
for nine decades you have roamed the Earth,
a quarter of a million miles
across every continent,
and we have been able to travel with you,
over land
under water
through the air
in awe and wonder
at the beauty of our living world.

Hail! David Attenborough, Sir
we have so much to be grateful for,
you opened our eyes
great silver-crowned king of Planet Earth.

Stare *

Murmuration, fascination,
swoop, glide, sail on your sea of cloud
black swirling waves,
moving patterns of aerial choreography
smartphones try to capture your beauty,
magic, improbability,
how many ‘likes’ today
for your eerie phenomenon?

Today over the Goosemarsh thousands soar,
did your ancestors fly here in Domesday
and our ancestors squint at the sky like us?
And when the builders scar our open land
will you still be there?
And people stare
through windows or outdoors
to be charmed, mystified, amazed.

Each bird with pointed bill
lively awkward walk, iridescent feathers
flock as one Sturnus Vulgaris,
rest, roost for the night
tomorrow repeat those graceful stunts
sweep and dive in unison,
whirl above our heads
your autumn twilight spectacle.

For your name is on the red critical list
eighty percent fall in numbers
the unbelievable truth
that the day may come when this marvel is no longer
the village gossip
but the stuff of myths and legends
and our only wonder will be
'What happened to the starlings?'

* *Stare - Old English for 'starling'. Replaced by the 16th Century*

Statistic

You laughed as your brother pulled faces
in the back of that overcrowded truck,
grasped your father's fingers to take your first steps,
together dodging puddles around the squalid camp,
giggled when your sister sang and clapped by the fire,
babbled your first words beneath a grubby tarpaulin
whilst your mother stirred a meagre supper,
played happily by the dribbling standpipe
splashing and squealing,
soon there would water and waves everywhere
as far as anyone could see.

Did your father agonize whether or not to journey onwards
when his dreams were punctured by reality?
Did your mother's hands tremble when she fastened
your over-sized lifejacket? Did she pray?
Did your brother and sister scramble aboard the rickety craft
shivering with cold or fear?
Did you nestle contentedly between them?

Artin, you only saw one winter.

The Nezhad family from Sardasht, West Azerbaijan attempted to cross the Channel on 27th October 2020. Artin's body was eventually found at Karmoy in Norway.

Sunflowers Will Turn Their Heads

The sunflowers will turn their heads
away from the light,
they will flower as they always do
acre upon acre
across a land of extinguished dreams,
green shoots of hope will push through
when the ground warms again,
tall strong stalks climb
circles of bright yellow petals
surround myriads of seeds,
but this year when the sun glows
over dazzling fields
and in abandoned cities
golden pear-shaped domes glisten
against blue summer skies,
the sunflowers will turn their heads
away from the light.

The sunflowers will turn their heads
to peer into their own shadows
painful farewells echo
simple joys now lost
amidst the chaos of a cruel exodus,
smoke and flames choke the skies

where blue and yellow flags fly in tatters,
bodies are buried hastily
in scorched earth,
yet unconquerable spirits haunt
the ruins of their beloved homeland,
anthems ring out across borders,
the sunflowers must bow their heads
in mourning for proud Ukraine.

The Dream of Ewan Corlett

Colony of Gentoo penguins
her curious companions,
Magellan snipe strut on rotting decks
long deserted by mariners,
unclaimed by the ocean
vast hole-riddled carcass condemned
to South Atlantic purgatory.

Picnic parties, feel free to take photos
whilst upland geese feed on your crumbs,
but I should warn you
she no longer has a ‘best side’
this rusting hulk in godforsaken cove
whose glory days
need to be remembered.

Trophy hunters steer clear,
do not salvage relics
lest the genius in the high hat
haunts you evermore,
He launched her, heard her hallowed
‘The greatest experiment
since the Creation.’

Illustrious Victory, Warrior, Cutty Sark,
I hear them, I hear them
calling her back
to British shores
eight thousand nautical miles
no matter, it can be done
it will be done.

Strange judgement you may say
to deem her worthy of resurrection,
madness my wife concludes,
time and tides have waited
noble S.S. Great Britain, first iron built
ocean-going steamship,
never underestimate my iron resolve.

Ship-shape and Bristol-fashion,
see them hoist the flags,
hear the cheers.

Written to mark the 50th Anniversary of the return of S.S. Great Britain from the Falkland Islands to the Bristol shipyard where she was built. Ewan Corlett, naval architect, masterminded her rescue.

The Spoils of War

It is both a blessing and a curse
to emerge alive
dazzled by the brightness of the morning,
like a mole when accidentally
pushing his head above ground,
for weeks we cowered in a basement,
now startled by the song of a solitary bird
perched high in a charred treetop,
howling missiles stole our springtime.

It is both with joy and with horror
I find my home
still stands amidst the chaos
four walls and a roof intact.
Bitter wind rips through
each shattered windowpane,
ransacked drawers tipped out
treasures hurriedly stuffed into pockets
invaders stole my prized possessions.

It is both in hope and in despair
I wait at the station
gazing at my phone screen,
see my airpods have crossed borders,
imagine my gold locket around
the neck of a laughing faraway girl,
while my precious infant sleeps in my arms
she has spent half her life in darkness
may hatred never steal her heart.

Thirteen

Into the cavernous gaping jaws
along the rocky gullet,
young adventurers clamber
through craggy mountains,
towards the cave of mysteries,
hearts racing with excitement.

Floodwater creeps menacingly
no turning back,
thirteen souls imprisoned
in the darkest dampest cell,
low hanging limestone
rough ledges, oozing mud.

Blacker than the night
eyes open eyes closed
indistinguishable darkness,
days and nights morph
into timeless terror
the World holds its breath.

Under the moonlight
faithful and faithless
together in prayer,
lighting candles for

comfort and consolation,
hope in the flicker of a flame.

In this race against time
floodlights illuminate
pumps, diving gear,
array of medical equipment,
United Nations together in
resourcefulness and ingenuity.

Shallow breathing
life is fading fast,
hands held in friendship
hands clasped in prayer
hands cupped to capture
life-saving droplets from the cave roof.

And then the incredible moment,
light glimmers through water
painfully dazzling huddled bodies,
a lone diver surfaces,
calls out "How many?"
"Thirteen"
.... the miracle begins.

Tham Luang Cave Rescue, Thailand June/July 2018

This Camping Lark

Looked around
chose our pitch,
put up the tent
without a hitch.
Ground's all bumpy
sleeping bag's lumpy.
Thinking of ditching this camping lark.

Camping cooker's okay
for the first day,
beans and sausage make a banquet
when you're shivering in a blanket,
Mum would love a cup of tea
forgot the sugar, don't blame me!
Thinking of ditching this camping lark.

Waterside site
looked all right.
Hey! levels are rising
hardly surprising
rain torrential
flooding potential!
Thinking of ditching this camping lark.

Wind howling all night
owl gave us a fright,
no one can sleep
mud six inches deep,
traipse to the toilet block,
now it's past one o' clock,
trudge back, pitch dark
where on earth did we park?
Thinking of ditching this camping lark.

Roof starts leaking
tent pole's creaking
neighbour's snoring
tried ignoring
turned on the lamp
everything's damp!
Thinking of ditching this camping lark.

Morning has broken
children have woken
"The sun's come out!"
they all shout
dew drops sparkle
wildflowers startle
fresh air to breathe
everything we need

brook is babbling

ducks are dabbling

steppingstones and wellies

beat cartoons on the telly,

bird song delights,

hungry appetites,

bacon sarnies all round

as we stretch out on the ground.

I think.....I'll just stick......with this..crazy..camping...lark.

Truth

Obedient rows
of bright Sunday school faces
gaze upwards,
rosaries clutched.
The truth is today we are learning about Sin.

Nuns circle, swoop,
hooded crows intent on their carrion,
sweet faces,
harsh words.
The truth is we want to go out to play.

How hot is hell? I wonder,
sunshine beckons through the high window,
what is Purgatory? I puzzle,
will my cat go to heaven? I worry.
The truth is seven-year-olds are very impressionable.

Dear Sister Agatha
knows all there is to know about Sin,
pure as the driven snow,
fragrant as spring blossom.
The truth is her confessions are over in a trice.

Listening to her words
I imagine ink blobs on blotting paper,
sins spidering about
blackening my soul.
The truth is eternal damnation is frightening.

On Sunday my scabby knees
are sore from kneeling for so long.
"Hurry up! You can't have been that bad"
whispers my mother impatiently.
The truth is I've lost count of my *'Hail Marys'*.

Devoted Sister Agatha
taught us so well the perils of evil,
the punishments.
But now I know the truth.
The truth is fear in childhood leaves its mark.

Unspoken

She never told me
where you were,
perhaps I never asked
that difficult question for
her so difficult to answer,
but once I thought
I saw you,
just a glimpse was enough
to place you safely somewhere,
that day our bus passed
a city cemetery
through the forest of headstones
one beautiful stone angel
wings outstretched
gently gazing downwards,
and I thought it may
just be the place
where you lay
flowers at your head
asleep in pink perfection
my little brother
two days young,
'Ours is the next stop'
she tugged at my sleeve
I never saw my mother cry
she never saw a child's grief.

Waiting for the Sumitomo Bank to Open

That day you remembered
to feed the stray cat
scatter crumbs for garden birds
kiss your wife's photo good morning
before heading to the city.

Summer sun crosses a clear sky
your seated shadow remains still
tired unsteady legs forever resting
walking stick in hand forever waiting
image etched into the bank's stone steps.

Scorched in sudden obscene blast
frail body, fading memory,
immortalised by cataclysmic flash
love, care, culture, busyness blown into oblivion,
one hundred thousand mornings.

Whale Watching

Glutinous coiled mass
spills out
from slashed underbelly
thirty-foot corpse
butchered by curious villagers
on the golden shores of Kapota.
Stench of ambergris repels,
thirteen pounds of obscene plastic in your gut
one hundred and fifteen cups
twenty-five carrier bags
two flip flops
one thousand pieces of plastic
in this hideous inventory,
once mighty and majestic
deep-diving submariner
brain larger than any on Earth
never again the sight of you torpedoing through the ocean
the size of you
the power
the wonder
the beauty
the brilliance.

White Chestnut

In history
we read and hear
the shattering of window glass on Kristallnacht,
we read and smell
the burning of books, ritual destruction,
we read and see that ominous sight, plumes of grey smoke
rising from sinister chimneys,
we learn of the atrocities of war.

And yet it is through the leaves of a teenage journal
we are transported,
feel the emotions.
We read and touch the soul
as a young girl holds a pen
hovering above blank pages
of an open diary,
her companion in isolation
her comfort in times of turmoil,
condemnation of the viral swarm of Nazism,
while outside a constellation of yellow stars is herded on the streets.

In Amsterdam, the secret annex,
slide back the bookcase,
step through into the ultimate lockdown,
two years of hiding
two years of fear.
Life on hold.
Freeze frame desires and dreams
of optimistic youth,
trapped like a bird in a cage.

Glimpsing the ancient white chestnut
through high attic windows,
changing each season,
sole precious contact with nature.
Nature knowing nothing
of racial torment.
Nature brings eternal hope.
'What's done cannot be undone', her silent song,
'but one can prevent it happening again'
Anne Frank's words wise beyond her years, shining a light in the darkest corner of the Holocaust.

With Or Without Guardian Angels

Today it seems a comforting proposition
a guardian angel
at seven I was not so sure.

The nurse ushers me into your room
as if there is not a moment to lose
I soon see why.

You are still, so very still
three hundred miles but I am here now,
thankfully I am here.

Palliative care, all neat and tidy
no tubes, no wires, silence, outside world
permitted to seep in through your window

Piebald grazing, wind brushing the wheat fields,
clear sky, early spring sunshine
wheeling gulls tell of the closeness of the sea.

Do I talk of times past, family, the weather?
Sing softly, or sit quietly
gently holding your hand?

Last time you told me you wanted
to go back to Italy, me too,
what is there to stop us now?

Arm in arm we stroll to Piazza San Marco
this early we have the place to ourselves
mosaics glitter in the sunlight.

Let's have coffee in the square, choose a table,
it'll be expensive, no matter
today we shall treat ourselves.

Due latte and a selection of cakes
per favore, the musicians strike up
lively violins, rich reedy piano accordion.

Glorious to be in Venice this morning,
let's take our time, relax
we shall not leave until the music stops.

ABOUT THE AUTHOR

Sandra Mary Chambers hails from Nottingham but made Penkridge in Staffordshire her home. Following a long career in education she volunteered her time with various charities. Sandra did not pick up her poetry pen until September 2017 after being inspired by Mel Wardle Woodend at a poetry workshop.

Her poems have been published in several anthologies. She has become an active member of the Stafford WORD poetry community, and Newcastle Stanza group. She enjoys participating in open mic. events, and judging poetry slams.

October 2021 was a high point. Sandra was invited to read a poem at the Wells Festival of Literature, and one of her poems was awarded second prize in the Frances Browne Festival of Literature Poetry Competition.

Sandra writes "Poetry has been a good friend in difficult times, and a satisfying hobby. Now by sharing my poetry I hope we can raise funds to benefit the patients in the Midland Centre for Spinal Cord Injuries".

THE MIDLAND CENTRE FOR SPINAL INJURIES

The Midland Centre for Spinal Injuries is part of the Robert Jones and Agnes Hunt Hospital NHS Foundation Trust in Oswestry, Shropshire. This centre of excellence serves a catchment of 10 million from the West Midlands, Cheshire, South Mersey, Mid and North Wales. It provides a life-long service to 3,500 patients and admits on average 380 patients per year.

The multi-disciplinary team provides assessment, treatment and education to patients with spinal cord injury. Support is also provided to partners and family members. A spinal cord injury causes paralysis, sensory impairment, a multi-system physiological impairment and malfunction, as well as psychological, social, financial, environmental and vocational effects.

The MCSI is dedicated to the management of spinal injuries, maximising neurological recovery and function, minimising complications and disability, and through follow up appointments after discharge, maintaining health, independence and a good quality of life.

DREAM WELL WRITING LTD

Dream Well Writing Ltd are Staffordshire based publishers of dyslexia friendly books – with worldwide distribution and an environmentally conscious ethos – founded in 2017 by Mel Wardle Woodend Staffordshire Poet Laureate 2019 – 2022.

Find out more about Dream Well at

http://dreamwellwriting.simplesite.com/

https://www.facebook.com/dreamwellwriting/

dreamwellwriting@gmail.com

Printed in Great Britain
by Amazon

86717285R00066